UNDER FULL SAIL

ONE OF THE LAST OF THE GREAT SEA QUEENS . . . The four-masted bark Abraham Rydberg,
Swedish nautical cadet training vessel, sailing into New York Harbor in 1940. Flags and national
colors painted on her topsides inform World War II warships that she is a neutral ship.

UNDER FULL SAIL

Photographs *by* **MORRIS ROSENFELD**

Commentary *by* **EVERETT B. MORRIS**

Englewood Cliffs, N. J. PRENTICE-HALL, INC.

Library of Congress Catalog Card Number: 57-11973

Printed in the United States of America

93566

Foreword

LOVERS OF YACHTING were provided with a rare treat when, a decade ago, Morris Rosenfeld presented in book form a group of his famous yachting photographs. Yachtsmen everywhere—and a not inconsiderable number of landsmen with an appreciation of the beauty which comes only from the sea—will welcome this new collection, a most generous reward for ten years of waiting.

In a manner equalled by none, Rosy, as he is affectionately known to his many friends and admirers, has captured with his cameras the real flavor, spirit and zest of sailing. The many excellent pictures of out-of-the-ordinary events reflect his singular faculty of being always in the right place at the right time.

One of Rosy's many fine qualities is his phenomenal weather sense; a feeling for knowing that the day will be a good one for yachting pictures. His presence aboard *Foto* around the starting line before a race is regarded by the contestants as an augury of good breeze and plenty of racing action.

It is difficult to express in words the beauty and spirit of these pictures. Their uniform quality makes it still more difficult to distinguish by particular praise one photograph or sequence over any other. Perhaps those pictures which capture the awesome majesty of the towering America's Cup yachts will find widest admiration. Or those of the modern ocean racers plowing white furrows into the sea will kindle excitement.

But, whatever the yachtsman's special preference, in the ease and comfort of his library he may turn the leaves of this volume, never tiring of the companionship of the pictures and of the memories they evoke. He will live again many of the pleasantest experiences of his life, feeling the lift and surge of a driving hull beneath him, enjoying the tang of the fresh sea breeze that blows through these pages.

The set and contour of perfectly fitting sails; the action of water and wave on the hull; the indescribable beauty of the sea, sky and clouds; close moments in a race; the technique of starts, maneuvers and tactics—all are preserved here to invite study, to encourage retrospection.

Rosy and his marvelous pictures will live long in the hearts of yachtsmen who share my deep gratitude for the pleasure that this book provides. I hope that the years will bring us many more collections of Rosy's yachting photographs: masterpieces of the master of *Foto* and her devoted, skillful crew—his sons.

CORNELIUS SHIELDS

Photographs

HALF A CENTURY and a bit ago, when sailing ships and shipyards that catered to them were still familiar to New York's teeming East River, Morris Rosenfeld made his first photograph.

It was a snapshot of a square-rigged vessel hauled out on a Houston Street slip, a picture made with a second-hand camera whose proprietorship he shared with several teen-age friends who had combined assets to effect its release from pawnshop bondage.

On that day the boy who had flirted with photography as a pastime metamorphosed into the youth who joined it in a devoted life partnership which was to bring rich rewards to both principals of this chance marriage of young art and dedicated artist.

For the picture won a prize. That prize provided the capital for the purchase of Rosy's first wholly owned camera and the impetus for an unparalleled career in the field of illustrative marine reporting.

Today Morris Rosenfeld stands virtually alone at the summit in this endeavor. The tens of thousands of pictures he has made since the fortuitous first one fill the galleries of classic ship and sea photography; his voluminous files form a comprehensive chronicle of sail in our time.

Who knows whether this would have eventuated if it had not been the very young Rosy's turn to have the camera, if he had not strolled down to Houston Street to feast his eyes on the ship, if his infallible instinct had not told him to aim his lens and click his shutter the moment that the sun broke through the clouds to bathe in beauty the sturdy, functional tracery of masts, yards, and rigging? Lesser quirks of Fate have shaped the courses of lesser lives.

I

The passage from struggling anonymity to recognized pre-emi-
nence was by no means all smooth sailing; but Rosy had—and still
has—the vital attributes for success in an avocation which became
his profession: exceptional native talent, the pride and integrity to
avoid the rocks and shoals of expediency, the business acumen to
weather economic storms, and the iron self-discipline of the perfectionist who is always striving for the best even in competition with
himself.

He left school at thirteen to do a man's work in a man's world,
armed only with the clumsy Gundlach 4 x 5 plate camera his five-
dollar prize had bought and a not very well-defined urge to be either
an artist or a star news photographer.

He worked for an old German who used to photograph on wood
and copper for textbook illustrations. He free-lanced for *Leslie's
Weekly* and *Harper's;* worked with Levick, the leading yacht photographer of those days; and studied art at Cooper Union.

The rough and tumble of a magazine and newspaper photographer's life proved more alluring to the young Rosenfeld than art as
such, and he soon abandoned his crayons and brushes. He covered
Tong wars in Chinatown, the finish of a sailing passage from Bermuda
to Atlantic City, a Chinese picnic at College Point; and he photo-
graphed blutwurst manufacture for the *Staats Zeitung.* He did the
fascinating variety of chores which are the lot of a big-city reporter,
working with lens and plate instead of pad and pencil.

In 1906 he married Esther Marion Hirsch, a bright-eyed, dark-
haired little lady who was his assistant, his inspiration, his under-
standing friend in the hard, uncertain early years of trying to get a
new business established.

This union produced four children: three sons, who became
yachtsmen and photographers without their father's trying to influ-
ence their choice of career; and a daughter, who married a sailing
enthusiast. Few families are more closely bound by a mutuality of
interests. Business and table talk always seems to center on yachts

and yachting, photographs and photographic equipment. And all speak with authority tempered by respect for the superior knowledge of the head of the clan.

It was in 1910 that Rosy opened his first office at 116 Nassau Street in downtown Manhattan. He is still there; but the establishment bears little resemblance to the original cubicle, whose door still carries this legend: MORRIS ROSENFELD, PHOTOGRAPHIC ILLUSTRATOR. Which is not unlike classifying Fritz Kreisler as a fiddler, or John Singer Sargent as an interior decorator.

No matter what sort of work he did for bread and butter, Rosy never neglected his first love, his real love, for sea and sky and ships. The more he worked with these subjects, the more the public wanted; so perhaps it was inevitable that he gradually came to specialize in marine photography, inevitable that he became the man who could say almost casually, "I have covered every major American yachting event since Sir Thomas Lipton came over here with his first *Shamrock* in 1899."

Floppy white canvas hat shading his alert, ranging, good-humored eyes; the stump of a cigar in the corner of his mouth; camera dangling from one hand while the other steadies the shoulder strap of his film magazine bag, Rosy is a familiar figure at yachting centers from Maine to Florida, on fresh water and salt. He never seems to be without camera or cigar. The latter is for relaxation, the former just in case he happens to see something of pictorial interest.

He likes to think of himself as a reporter and would be genuinely embarrassed if it were suggested that his work entitled him to be called the Winslow Homer or Gordon Grant of the camera.

Actually, he is that happy combination of reporter and artist. In Rosy the line between them is indiscernible because his work, even on what are basically routine assignments, is a characteristic blend of reportorial accuracy, the highly polished photographic technique of the skilled craftsman, and the artist's sensitivity to color and line and mood.

The perfectionist in him is never more obvious than when he is stalking a subject from the cockpit of his fast, highly maneuverable little cruiser *Foto*. He sometimes will follow a yacht, or group of several yachts, for an hour or more, squinting through the finder from time to time and then setting the camera down again without triggering the shutter until that one fleeting, perfect instant arrives when sun, sail, wave, and cloud all get together to pose what he regards as a picture worth taking.

Something less, a good deal less, would have satisfied the editor or the boat-owner who had given him the assignment, but it would not have satisfied Rosy. Therein lies one of the clues to his success. If a photograph is to appear with the credit line, "Photo by Morris Rosenfeld," it is going to be the best possible picture he could make under the conditions, or it won't appear.

This emphasis on quality would have less meaning, of course, if Rosy were not the master craftsman. Perhaps no one is more aware and respectful of his reportorial genius—he always seems to be where something newsworthy is happening—and of his ability to produce results that are the envy and despair of imitators, than are his three sons. All are expert photographers in their own right and knowledgeable in the sport of sailing; but there are occasions when they are still pupils in the severe, practical school conducted by the master himself at a stage of his career when he would be more than justified in shifting the load to the shoulders of the logical heirs to his mantle. Retirement simply never interests a healthy, active man whose vocation and avocation are one and the same.

Stanley, the second boy, says this of the family's photographic operations: "There is a delightful competitiveness in working with Dad. He never has forgotten that he used to be a newspaperman, and he delights in scoring a beat on us."

William, the youngest, will tell you, "When we go out on a job together, we might take a dozen pictures to Dad's one. We will wind up with a dozen acceptable exposures. Dad will have the picture."

No one is more appreciative of the Morris Rosenfeld tradition, the vast scope of his father's work and its surpassing quality, than David, the first son. His was the monumental task of inspecting thousands of Rosy's best pictures to select a few hundred prospective subjects for inclusion in this book and then toil with the writer in deciding upon the comparative handful that could be woven into the fabric of this tapestry of sailing.

Amateur camera enthusiasts without number admire his work and aspire to approach it in their own efforts. They importune him frequently for advice on yachting photography, and he gives it freely. What he cannot give the supplicants is that indefinable quality, that combination of technique, timing, good taste, and deep-lying appreciation of the inherent beauty of sail and sea that is the Rosenfeld hallmark.

"How do you do it?" they ask. "What sort of a camera do you use, what kind of film, what filter, what developer?"

Patiently, he provides answers based on his own incomparable experience. He explains that the camera used for one photograph may not be suitable for the next, that the film used today may not be the one used tomorrow, that the only filter he likes is the pale yellow one because he dislikes "arty" effects.

"Fifty years ago," he tells them, "cameras were 6½ x 8½, or larger, and we used plates. Today's cameras are generally 4 x 5, or smaller, and film is used exclusively. The slow orthochromatic or 'color blind' emulsions have given way to fast panchromatic emulsions. The old pyro developer, which had to be mixed before each use, has been replaced by a fine-grain developer, which keeps indefinitely.

"I have seen many changes in my time and have tried to keep up with all that might help me in my work. But one thing has never changed: that is, it is much more important to concentrate on the photograph itself rather than worry about the details of exposure, filter, and film.

"The trick is to establish as a reflex action the mechanics of the camera you are using and keep the mind free to size up the picture in front of you. The types of equipment and material used are not nearly so important as the mastery of them."

So speaks the master technician himself, a craftsman equally at home with 4 x 5, 5 x 7, or the 2¼ x 3¼. He can shoot his quarry with either with equal facility, whether he is firing from the solid platform of a wharf or from the lively, mobile perch provided by *Foto*.

In the latter connection, he gives full marks to his sons, who steer the boat and operate its throttle and clutch controls while he is concentrating on making the picture.

"That is why my best photographs are made from my own boat while one of the family is skipper," he says. "The boys not only know how to run the boat, but also know just what I have in mind when I go out to get good action shots at starts and at the turns, to get onto film tactical sequences and interesting situations."

Then there are other considerations: the necessity for keeping the distance between subject and object constant, keeping the angle of view the same, and anticipating with the photographer just when sea and sails look best.

"And that isn't all the boys and I have to do out there in *Foto*," Rosy adds. "While all this is going on we must be on the alert for other photographic possibilities in the vicinity and keep from interfering with anyone. It is quite a job."

Just how well the Rosenfeld team has done it is a matter of record, a record from which many glowing, glorious pages have been extracted to make this book.

THE SEA IS A THEATER, on whose restless stage only the actors change. Scenery, painted in Nature's incomparable studios, is immutable. Presentations, be they tragedy, melodrama or pure spectacle, are played from the same classic scripts. But ships, the stars who lend their brilliance and glamor to these works, inevitably fade into the offstage shadows, doomed by Time and modernism's march, never again to bow to acclaim in the proscenium's glare.

Because this is so, there are sights that the older among us will never see again and that younger eyes have never so much as glimpsed :

...   The fantastic Class J sloops racing for the America's Cup, their masts stretching fourteen stories upward toward the sky's illimitable roof.

...   Great three-stickers, like the schooners *Atlantic* and *Migrant,* tearing through the water faster than some steamships.

...   Wonderful, beautiful *Vanitie,* sporting three different rigs in the course of her bridesmaid's career.

...   Fleets of Nat Herreshoff's early-twentieth-century creations blotting out the clouds with their broad gaff-headed mainsails and the inverted triangles of their club topsails.

The pageant of sailing lost some of its majesty, some of its grandeur and not a little of its romance with their passing.

But because Rosy the reporter, Rosy the artist, Rosy the discerning historian was there with his omnipresent camera to record their triumphs, their disappointments, their varying moods, the great players in the great shows of sailing's age of canvas and wood and hemp perform again in these pages.

All are here: old troupers in their frills and furbelows treading the wind's path to establish the tradition being carried on today by younger, slicker performers in the habiliments of modern functionalism.

Square yards, topsail clubs and thrusting jibbooms have all but disappeared from the sailing scene. So, too, have the spider webs of ratlined shrouds and the stacks of wooden hoops that carried the tarred luff ropes of working canvas up and down solid, heavy masts that once had been tall, straight trees.

Bowsprits, if you see them nowadays, are stubby versions of the proud sticks that flaunted the headsails of the old flyers. This is the day of snug, inboard rigs; of airplane-metal spars and hollow, built-up masts. Gleaming rods of stainless steel, or wire of the same material, have replaced the thicker, clumsier cables that stayed the spars of earlier yachts. Bronze slides and tracks have done away with mast hoops, and no sturdy gaff stretches the head of the now completely conventional triangular main or mizzen sail.

Hemp and canvas have yielded in sail and boatswain's lockers to nylon and dacron and other synthetics. We've had ships of bronze, iron and steel and ships of wood. We still have them. But advances in metallurgy and chemistry are giving us hulls of thin, strong aluminum and one-piece shells fashioned from sheets of glass fiber bonded in plastic.

Sailing, for all that it is anachronistic as a means of water transportation, is anything but static. The modern ocean-going cruising yacht is as much of an advance over the heavy, lumbering little off-shore vessels of half a century ago as the tea clippers and Liverpool packets were over the caravels of Columbus and the *Mayflower* of the Pilgrims.

The evolution has been recorded pictorially by Rosy. He tells the story of change accurately, but not without a touch of sentiment and nostalgia. He bridges three generations of sail in these pages and does it with the deft, sure touch of the master.

WINDJAMMERS OF THIS ILK were the prototypes of the large sailing yachts of an era whose end was hastened by the conflict that embroiled the world from 1939 to 1945. The lines, rigging and accommodation of the prosaic commercial vessel were refined to produce the luxuriously appointed, breathtaking lovely ships that not so very long ago were the pride and flower of America's yachting fleet.

The old coasting schooners and the trans-oceanic square-riggers worked hard and lived dangerously until cargoes could no longer be found for them to carry. Then they retired to quiet backwaters to become pitiable hulks, or to rot away in idleness like laborers become too old and weary and ill to toil.

Their more glamorous sisters from the yachting side of the tracks also knew popularity, fame and good fortune in their heyday; did their duty as patrol or training vessels in World War II and then, all but forgotten by their once fawning admirers, fell upon evil times.

SHADOW AND SUBSTANCE and symbolism—in this study of clewed-up sails on the foremast yards of a square-rigged ship starkly outlined against a cloudless sky.

10

ONE OF THE LAST of the down-Easters was the Daniel Getson. Heavily laden, topsides scarred and rust-streaked, patched sails darkened with age, the old three-masted coastwise cargo schooner slips down Long Island Sound, setting everything she can to help her along in the gentle breeze.

MOONLIGHT'S SOFT, SILVERY TOUCH lends an aura of romantic beauty to this scene, one which may never be repeated in these waters. The Daniel Getson may have been one of this group of working schooners riding to their anchors off City Island, awaiting tugs and pilots to take them up the East River to berths in the shadow of steel and concrete skyscrapers.

MIGRANT IS THE EPITOME of sleek, well-groomed efficiency as she sails close-hauled up a nice, pleasant breeze. In those happy days she flew the private signal of Carll Tucker. Later she served in the U. S. Coast Guard. And now, stripped of her long bowsprit and tall spars, her once dazzling deck enclosed in an ugly wooden house, she is a Central American banana boat, a Caribbean cargo-carrying drudge.

MAID OF ENGLAND, one of the last of the square-riggers to bring a cargo to New York. Rosy happened along as she was making her approach, and two of the barkentine's crew climbed out to the end of her jibboom to watch him make this historical photograph.

14

THE PROUD ATLANTIC, *blue-ribbon holder on the ocean for which she was named, was one of the loveliest yachts ever built and certainly one of the fastest. In 1905, this 185-foot vision of symmetry in sail and hull, won the Kaiser's Cup in a race from Sandy Hook to The Lizard in twelve days and fourteen hours, a record unequalled or surpassed by any vessel under sail. She, too, served the Coast Guard, part of the time under a staysail rig between her masts, and then was sold down the river. Now, stripped of her lead, she sits in the mud of the New Jersey Intracoastal Waterway—no longer proud, no longer lovely, eking out an existence as a roadside tearoom.*

A SIGHT TO THRILL even the most jaded connoisseur of sailing beauty is the full-rigged ship Seven Seas, a familiar favorite of camera enthusiasts when she was sailing out of Oyster Bay before the war.

SLIDING DOWN THE BACK of a long ocean roller is the ship Tusitala, sailing before a faint, following air, barely strong enough to keep her canvas asleep. Like Seven Seas, she is no longer on the yacht register.

THE WIZARD OF BRISTOL, as the late Nat Herreshoff was known in tribute to his genius as a naval architect and engineer, was an established titan in his field of endeavor before Rosy began his long climb up the stony road to recognition. Yet these two artists, one the creator of fine yachts, the other a marine portraitist who recorded them for posterity on plate and film, were contemporaries during the period when American yachting attained much of its glory and perhaps its greatest development.

Typical of the Herreshoff racing yachts of the early part of the century were the nine sloops built to the New York Yacht Club 50-Foot Class in 1913, at the now incredible price of $17,000 each.

SQUARED AWAY before the wind, and preparing to set old-fashioned tall, narrow spinnakers to spill air into big balloon jibs are these three Fifties. Modern parachutes do the work of spinnaker and ballooner and do it better.

EIGHT YEARS LATER, in 1921, still with the original rig, Acushla (later Revery) and Istalena cross on their way up to the windward mark.

AND FORTY-THREE YEARS LATER, here is Pleione, one of the original glamor girls of the class, as chesty with her huge bubble of a spinnaker as an Italian movie actress in a strapless evening gown. She's schooner-rigged now and, despite her advanced years, still winning major trophies.

LAST OF THE BIG RACERS were the yawls Manxman (left) and Thistle. Herreshoff built the steel Manxman (then Katoura) in 1927 and designed and constructed the bronze-hulled Thistle a year later. Here the rivals, their sails soaked from the black rain squall that has just passed over them, are having one of their typical close brushes. For several years after World War II, they lent their grace and dignity to the New York Yacht Club cruising squadron. Then they were sold out of the country, Manxman to Venezuela, Thistle to Turkey, as naval cadet training vessels.

23

VANITIE NEVER MADE IT as an America's Cup defender, but she was as lovely and interesting a yacht as sailed in her days—plural because she crowded three different careers into her quarter-century of life. As a typical gaff-headed, club-topsailed sloop of that era, she was an unsuccessful candidate for the assignment of defending the mug against the challenge of Sir Thomas Lipton's *Shamrock IV*. In the mid-twenties she was transformed into a schooner and raced in that rig. Come 1930 and another challenge from Sir Thomas, *Vanitie* came out with a shorter bowsprit and a tall, modern jib-headed sail plan to serve as a trial horse for the four new defense candidates. A few years later, when no one was any longer interested in trying to maintain racing yachts of her size, her all-bronze hull was bought by a shipbreaker.

VANITIE *IN HER FIRST DRESS, ghosting along in air that hardly ripples the water which absorbs the shadow of her sails.*

STYLES CHANGED and so did Vanitie. Here she is as a schooner, flying a main-topmast balloon staysail between her masts.

AT THE AGE OF SIXTEEN, Vanitie had a whole new outfit. In 1930 she was this beautifully turned-out playmate of cup defenders.

AND HERE SHE IS, a big white bone in her teeth, lee rail down in a smother of foam, bowling along on a close reach (see page 26).

THEY WERE HUGE AND EXPENSIVE, but the Class J sloops that raced for the America's Cup in 1930, 1934 and 1937 were nothing if not photogenic. Rosy has preserved for us all of the power and beauty and dignity which awed those lucky enough to have seen them in their very short racing lives. Economic conditions, which forced a new way of yachting life on even the wealthiest Americans, made these glamor girls of the sport easy prey for the shipbreakers.

LAST OF THE SHAMROCKS *was number five on the list of Sir Thomas Lipton's unsuccessful challengers for the antique silver ewer.*

LAST AND GREATEST of the defenders was Ranger *(see page 28), the third yacht sailed in cup matches by Harold S. Vanderbilt. Nothing could touch her. She's carrying a double-clewed, quadrilateral jib, a sail now barred by rules from ocean racers.*

ENDEAVOUR I CAME CLOSEST to taking the cup back to Britain. She's flying her perforated spinnaker, an aerodynamic experiment.

RAINBOW, ONLY NEW BOAT built for 1934 defense, had rod rigging and flexible boom. She beat Endeavour I *after losing two races.*

YANKEE *LOVED IT* when the breeze piped up. Here she is, with double-clewed genoa jib, splitting a wave into twin clouds of spray. She failed of selection as defender twice.

AND *SHE COULD GO DOWN-HILL, TOO,* under the pull of this tremendous Mae Westian spinnaker.

THE FIRST CHALLENGE from England since 1937 was on behalf of a yacht of the International 12-Meter Class, a few units of which are now the largest purely racing-type sloops still active in this country. They are shorter in overall length than the Class J boats were on the water, and the rules governing cup competition had to be changed for their benefit.

SCENES LIKE THIS will be repeated in 1958 when trials are held to select cup defender. Three Twelves (left to right) Nereus, Vim and Nyala—having a close tussle on Long Island Sound.

SHE'LL BE AN ASPIRANT for selection. Twelve-meter sloop Vim, newest and fastest of American Twelves, would seek to defend the cup. Shade and sunlight do things for her.

THE START IS THE THING when championship chips are down. Even a very fast boat finds it difficult to recover if she is buried in the backwind of a big fleet at the getaway gun. A long, properly angled starting line helps the contestants immeasurably in their quest for nicely spaced, clear-wind positions. These pictures show aspirants for the Comet Class Mid-Winter championship making that kind of a start on that kind of a line on Biscayne Bay.

GUN! The starting signal is hoisted, the gun fired and sheets trimmed in as the fleet comes onto the wind for a well-aligned start. Number 2909, nearest flag, is slow flattening down her main but has best position.

TEN SECONDS TO GO, and all but a couple of stragglers are easing up to the line with jibs and mainsails slacked off to kill speed. No one wants to be over too soon.

HAVING RUN STARTING LINE all the way down to the committee boat, *Three Belles* has to tack to clear its bow. She does so. But, Oops! There's someone heading for her with right of way on the starboard tack (just to right of Number 10, which is in process of coming about). So-o-o-o . . .

AND HERE'S a not-so-good start—in fact, a disastrous one—for *Three Belles* (Number 22) as International One-Designs start Manhasset Bay Yacht Club race in lively Long Island Sound breeze.

THREE BELLES *(top, page 37) quickly flops back onto starboard tack and, with little way on, tries to squeeze between Aries (Number 8) and the committee boat's bow. But, Oops! again—the latter's long anchor line is in the way. Three Belles luffs up to avoid it, almost hits Aries and gets all aback.*

SAGGING DOWN ON AN-chor line and along it to the committee boat's bow, where strong - armed committeeman tries to fend her off. That's all for poor Three Belles this day. Having fouled the committee boat, her race is over before it has begun. Aries, which has had her troubles, too, finally wriggles clear.

SPECTACULAR, CLOSE-QUARTERS STARTS are the rule rather than the exception when red-hot racing classes go off to the sailing wars. Witness these examples of the International Stars and International One-Designs hitting the starting line with split-second accuracy under quite different conditions of wind and water.

WITH FINE MILITARY PRECISION, the huge fleet racing for the North American Star Class championship swings across the line and trims sheets for a beat up a gentle wind to the first mark.

STILL SHOULDER TO SHOULDER (rail to rail, that is), after nearly three miles of windward work, the three leaders arrive at the turning buoy.

MARCHING UP TO THE LINE like well-drilled troops, the
IOD's are off on a fast climb up a spanking breeze.

CUTTING IT FINE, perhaps too fine, is boat nearest flag marking lee end of starting line. Tense crew watches flag and strains ears for crack of gun.

RIDING THE RAILS is all in a windy day's work for crews of International One-Designs when there's a slog to windward ahead. The purpose is the same—to keep the boat on its "feet"—but railbirds have different techniques.

HOLD EVERYTHING, MATE! Tumbler on rail of port tack boat is close to tumbling overboard, as his skipper puts helm up to bear away under Number 22's stern.

THE CLINGING VINE STYLE, exemplified by crew of Dodger,
one *tendril* on deck, other hooked over the side.

NOT AN ABANDON SHIP DRILL, feet foremost, but Arthur Knapp's Bumble Bee crew draping itself over the weather side.

SURF (NUMBER 21) uses clinging vine method, while Myyen's (Number 6) railriders try it side-saddle.

LOOKS LIKE a railriders' convention.
Only one dissenter to "everyone-up-
everyone-out" motion.

46

WHILE SPRAY FLIES in all directions, this crew demonstrates combination of casual drape and rigidly formal methods of hiking out for benefit of equally wet but less acrobatic pursuers.

SMOOTH AS A MIRROR, and as reflective, is the sea in its occasional quiet moods. In this situation crews sit stiffly still, or move slowly and gingerly as they go about their duties. They even talk in whispers lest they disturb what little air is stirring in their sails as the boats ghost down to the turning buoy.

CALMS ARE NOT DISCRIMINATING. *They take classes that have started as much as twenty-five minutes apart and blend them into one slow-moving, unhappy group. Here's a mixed bag of cruisers and racers, reflections of their sails shimmering on the softly wrinkled, glassy surface of the Sound— making a pretty, if somewhat pussy-footed, descent on a motionless, and consequently silent, bell buoy.*

LUCKY LITTLE FLICA gets around the buoy ahead of what is going to be an horrendous traffic jam. After a period of calm, which caused classes to drift together, a new breeze comes in astern, piles everyone up in heaps, inspires frantic cries of "Room! Room at the mark!" and produces no end of unhappiness among those forced to the outside of the big turning circle. But it is all in a day's racing on Long Island Sound.

DROOPING SPINNAKERS reflect the discouragement of these Lightning Class sailors as clearly as the water returns the images of mainsails, on which the class insigne now seems inappropriate.

*THERE MAY BE WIND in those clouds above this jumble of Atlantics, Herre-
shoff "S" boats and Stars fighting their way up to and around a mark hidden
somewhere in the log jam of hulls and canvas. There had better be, or this
pack will never make it home before the race time limit expires.* 51

O UT OF BRIGHT SKIES and leaden, the wind can blow with equal vigor, making crews pay in physical contortions and discomfort for fast passages.

THERE'S MORE OF THIS COMET out of the water than there is in it, and more of its crew overboard than on board; purely a matter of cause and effect, of balance and counterbalance. The helmsman is giving "one hand for the ship" (specifically the tiller) and desperately keeping the other for himself. Chances are, too, that he's enjoying himself—or thinks that he is.

FOUR DEUCES ON THE SAIL (see page 54) and two damp jacks on the rail, as this Star boat, gleaming white against dark sky and darker water, slashes to windward.

IN ANY SORT OF WEATHER Jean Blanchard (see page 55) was one of the best Snipe skippers on Long Island Sound. Here, perched on the rail while her shipmate keeps the mainsheet flat and gets his weight outboard, Jean steers Gala up the iridescent path of the westering sun.

"OUT OF THE DARK a new day flowers." Nature paints a panorama of tumbling water and cloud-streaked sky, frames it with the rail and rigging of a sailing vessel and titles it simply: "Sunrise at Sea."

LUDERS SIXTEENS are only small boats, but on a day like this there's always room for one more—on the rail, at least—especially if he's muscular and heavy.

57

IT ISN'T ALWAYS fair weather, but the sailorman takes the good with the bad—and vice versa—and makes the best of all of it. For instance:

RIDING IT OUT in comfort is this Luders Sixteen Class sloop caught in a blinding, driving rain squall that flattens out the sea and makes its surface hiss and "smoke." She'll need a new jib, though. The one she left up there to flog about in the wind has begun to come apart at the clew.

BREEZING ON and getting too much for full sail. So the crew of Mustang, former flagship of the Cruising Club of America, ties reef into main while sloop slogs along under jib alone.

IT'S THICK OUTSIDE—and inside, too—but crews of these cruising yachts, snugged down and nested in a comfortable anchorage, can enjoy themselves while waiting for the fog to lift.

60

THE GLOOM of a drenching squall and the freshly washed white of the Star boat l'Etoile's deck contrast starkly as she runs for home while other yachts are still thrashing upstorm to the finish.

LOTS OF RAIN and not much wind in this squall. Luders Sixteens carry on and hope that the aftermath won't be a flat calm.

UNPERTURBED by the menacing bulk of the dark nimbus cloud, blotting out the higher, brighter alto cumulus, is New London Light, standing her watch at the mouth of the Thames on a forbidding summer morning.

AS YAWL ANCHORITE *meets*
a Gulf Stream sea . . .

As EACH untrammeled wave
rises before her, she
bursts upon it, scattering it into
whiteness to either side..."

she bursts upon it . . .

scattering whiteness to either side . . .

then dips into the valley before climbing to meet the next.

COMING EVENTS CAST THEIR SHADOWS. It won't be long now before bigger, faster staysail schooner *Nina* overtakes sloop *Gesture* and surges past her to windward (see page 68).

THE SHADOW of Nina's rig is already making ominous splotches on Gesture's mainsail.

FIDDLE-DE-DEE and Ho-Hum. An oily swell and no breeze makes sailing life a bore for Windigo. Even her very light-drifting headsail flounces as she dips her bow in a curtsy to the inevitable.

THE REPORTER sees them this way: each boat a separate, clearly defined entity.

THROUGH the same lens, but with different eyes, we see *Gypsy* pursuing two rivals on a spinnaker reach.

THE ARTIST draws them as a receding series of curves and planes.

BREATHTAKING BEAUTY, DAINTY GRACE and brute power. The chance of combining these in one picture of an ocean-racing yacht bowling along under the pull of a bulging parachute spinnaker is a challenge to the skill and artistry of any marine photographer. It is a challenge that few can resist and even fewer can meet successfully. Rosy is one of the select. Here are three of his masterpieces, each interpreting a different mood of sea and sky and movement, each emphasizing one of the three basic elements.

HERE IS POWER, straining, harnessed power, in the straight lines of her spar, the gentle curves of her sails and even in the foaming curl of her hissing wake as Lutine, the Lloyd's of London yawl, reels off the knots with all of her light sails set and drawing to a fresh breeze over the port quarter.

THE CREAMING BOW WAVE of the yawl Good News (see page 74) reflects the pulling power of her balloon fore-staysail and its embracing spinnaker, as she surges along in pursuit of the British yawl Bloodhound, smartly stepping out in her varicolored sailing costume.

A CLASSIC STUDY of varying cloud formations and the bubbling, molten-metal look of a sun-drenched sea mounts this portrait of a noble lady of the yachting realm (see page 75). Escapade, once queen of the Great Lakes, now a princess of the Pacific, moves with regal dignity down a gentle summer breeze.

DOWN TO THE SEA IN SHIPS in ever-increasing and enthusiastic numbers go America's young. No phase of the sport of sailing is growing more rapidly, more sturdily, more universally than junior racing. Tots and teen-agers by the thousands, organized into junior yacht clubs with their own fleets and flag officers, or grouped into sailing classes under paid and volunteer instructors, are learning knots and splices, customs and traditions of the sea, racing rules and tactics and how to take care of themselves afloat.

No one section of the United States has anything remotely resembling a monopoly on this activity. It flourishes on salt water and fresh, on rivers and ponds, on man-made lakes, on the seacoasts, in the hills and mountains and on the prairies—wherever there is water enough to float a boat.

On western Long Island Sound, where the small fry are more numerous than in any other yachting center (more than 1,200 are enrolled in the Junior Yacht Racing Association), their regattas frequently draw more contestants than do those of their elders. The wear and tear on sails, on paint and topsides and on the nerves of their tutors is great; but the youngsters enjoy themselves hugely, and many grow up to become instructors in their own right and thus help to perpetuate the happy breed.

ISN'T THIS GREAT FUN? The little girl who is sailing with the two seriously intent lads in this speeding Thistle is casting her vote in the affirmative with a happy grin.

NO SPOT FOR A CLAUSTROPHO-
bia sufferer is the congested area
around the turning mark, smoth-
ered by the clutter of canvas, in the
middle of this picture. While junior
instructors in the launches in the
foreground watch the proceedings
with a mixture of anxiety, exasper-
ation and resignation, their charges
revel in this apparently hopeless
jumble of Blue Jays, Meteors, Tech
dinghies and Penguins.

THE TANGLE UNRAVELS ITSELF
somehow, bit by bit, boat by boat.
Here we have the same scene a
minute or so later. One after another, the contestants extricate
themselves from potentially—and,
not infrequently, actually—illegal
situations, squeeze around the bob-
bing buoy and square away before
the feeble breeze before precipi-
tating another such Main Street
rush-hour jam at the next turn in
the course.

79

THE ACROBATIC, railriding crew of Bijope has this Lightning Class sloop "on her feet" and well to windward of the opposition. Not a very comfortable way to sail a boat, but definitely effective.

IT ISN'T ALWAYS SCRAMBLING in light-going for the junior yachtsmen. They have their days of lively sailing in good breezes on wide waters, days when young blood tingles with the excitement of making a little boat step along at close to its maximum hull speed under the conditions.

SHIPWRECKS, JUNIOR STYLE. It happens now and again in the best-regulated junior sailing regattas: a sudden squall, too tight a mainsheet, too slow a response by the helmsman and, Whoops! Over go the little boats and their crews. No real danger, though. Rescuers are at hand, the youngsters can swim and they've been taught to don lifejackets and stay with the boat in such emergencies. It is learning the hard way, but chances are that, after this experience, the young mariners won't make the same mistake again.

RESCUE NUMBER 1. Bill Luders' cruiser, You'll Do, *out of Stamford, Connecticut, moves into position to pluck two lads from their capsized* Blue Jay *and take it in tow. The captain, in the striped shirt, pins his attention on* You'll Do. *His shipmate, whose wristwatch may or may not be waterproof, looks questioningly at Rosy's* Foto, *which happened along to record the incident.*

RESCUE NUMBER 2. Foto does something besides transport Rosy and his cameras. A moment after making a picture of You'll Do's salvage operation, Foto came upon these swamped, anxious little dinghy sailors. "Throw us a line, Mister," shouts the boy in the checkered shirt through chattering teeth. No sooner said than done. Not one line, but two come snaking to skipper and crew from Foto's cockpit, and in a trice they'll be hauled aboard, rubbed dry and wrapped in warm blankets.

F RUSTRATION IS PART AND PARCEL of a sailorman's life: there always seems to be too much of something, or too little.

WHEN THE RAIN GOES PITTER-PATTER, the sea goes flatter, so does the wind and so, consequently, does the bedraggled spinnaker of this Luders Sixteen. Raindrops plopping into the water and the reflection of the dripping mainsail make an unusual picture; but the crew is not concerned with aesthetics—there's too much rain.

TOO MUCH AND TOO LITTLE: too much traffic, too little sea room and visibility for this big American President Line freighter harried in her passage up the Long Island Sound steamer channel by an entire racing class and a misty rain squall—an example of why shipmasters acquire gray hair early in their seafaring careers.

THE EFFECT IS THE SAME, only this time it is a case of too little—much too little wind. Holding the main boom out, the spinnaker up and the helm steady, the crew of the International 5.5-Meter yacht Little Flica is in the mood to trade lots of sunshine for a bit of breeze.

DOWN EAST. Late afternoon sun bathes this peaceful scene in a Maine harbor. Lobster pots on the pier are as typical of the country as rugged fishing boats and the rocky, evergreen-clad shore.

ETUDE. Characteristic of Rosy, the artist, is his ability to see—and catch—the intrinsic beauty of the commonplace. This study of the play of sunlight and shadow around the bow of an old but recently painted sailing hooker is a case in point. Workaday gear like bobstay chains, links of the anchor cable and the spare hook snugged up to the hawse hole have a romantic appeal to Rosy when their plainness is relieved by touches of silver from the sun's brilliant brush.

87

NO ROOM TO SPARE, as yawl Baruna and larger yawl Manxman, hard on the wind, squeeze past the tide-swept rip-rap at the foot of Race Rock Lighthouse, guardian of the western portal of Fishers Island Sound. Lightkeeper on railed balcony enjoys the spectacle to which his charge makes a stately contribution. He will never see a repetition of this imposing, suspenseful scene—Baruna is now on the Pacific Coast, Manxman in Central America.

A SPINNAKER is defined in nautical glossaries as "a light sail of great spread used on yachts when running before the wind."

Frequently it is described otherwise, with deep feeling and picturesque saltiness, by foredeck men whose duties have familiarized them with the capricious temperament of this most photogenic of sails.

A spinnaker is a thing of beauty, but no joy forever. Its moods are as unpredictably changeable as those of a spoiled movie star—and as varied. Comedy, drama, mystery, broad farce: it plays them all.

In its tractable, cooperative moments, the spinnaker is a vision of utilitarian loveliness: a curvacious, bosomy bundle of fluff performing its work quietly and efficiently with hardly a flutter of silken eyelids; a witch to beguile landsman and sailorman alike.

But its capacity for mischief is unlimited, its propensity for whimsy well known to all sailormen who have writhed in frustration as a synthetic cloud has inexplicably and inextricably wrapped itself around the headstay to form a pulsating hourglass whose shimmering symmetry is entirely unappreciated by an embarrassed crew.

Its power is awesome and commands respect: a huge bubble of nylon pulling tons of boat through the water with the ease of a locomotive drawing an empty freight car down a long grade; a wild thing swinging and thrashing about in a breeze as though possessed of demons; a relentless force heaving the yacht down on her beam ends, threatening to shake the rig out of her with every convulsive, shuddering tug.

Devoted, competent servant, calm and unruffled; whimsical, jittery jade; wretched, boisterous brawler; buoyant, bouffant beauty—

all of these and more is a spinnaker to those whose job it is to harness the power of one, to tame its temperament with pole and sheet and lift and guy.

INSIGNIFICANT, almost Lilliputian, looks the deckhand beneath the dark, bulging cloud that is the 12-meter sloop Zio's spinnaker.

WATCHMAN, WHAT OF THE KITE? Sailor sitting on foredeck, his eyes peering aloft, will keep afterguard informed as to how spinnaker is drawing during the long stern chase ahead.

SCHOONERS ARE NOT AT THEIR BEST under spinnakers, but that does not prevent them from contributing gems to the gallery of light sails art.

NINA FLIES HER KITE with a big reaching jib, a combination which dwar the sailor out on the bowsprit trying to do something about the foot of t jib chafing on the spinnaker sheet.

AGAINST A BACKGROUND OF SNOWY CUMULUS, Bounding Home *makes a cloud of her own with golliwobbler (main-topmast balloon staysail, to give it its full name) and spinnaker in matching curls.*

94

"BREAK HER OUT!" cries the man forward, as he steadies the spinnaker pole with one hand and takes a strain on the forward guy with the other. It is an off-the-wind start, and the quicker Golden Hind's kite bursts out of its stops the faster she'll go.

ONLY ONE SPINNAKER, but the effect of two is obtained by Ben Bow, which furled all of her working canvas and left the job of pulling her across a benign Gulf Stream to golli-wobbler and kite. Perfectly trimmed, they're doing it, and quite rapidly, too.

97

BIG TY" (the ketch *Ticonderoga*), with her half-bulwarked decks, carved clipper bow and golden eagle over her sternboard, is one of the most characterful and distinctive yachts in the cruising fleet.

"BIG TY" AND A BIG SEA *teamed up to make this picture of a rig without a ship. The huge swell, which rolled the light breeze out of the crumpled spinnaker and set the odd "mule" to slatting between the main backstay and bare mizzenmast, completely obscures Ticonderoga's long hull.*

WITH GRACE AND DIGNITY befitting one of her mature years, "Big Ty" slips gently down a light breeze toward an afternoon sun that bathes the sea in silver and heightens the whiteness of her busy light sails.

BUT LIFE IS NOT ALWAYS SO PEACEFUL, so lovely for Ticonderoga. *In another race, under windier skies, the tack of her spinnaker jumps out of the fitting holding it to the pole, and quickly the sail became a useless, contorted mass of fabric.*

AN INSTANT LATER, "Big Ty's" crew is getting the situation under control. The sheet is being brought aboard, hands are standing by the halyard and another is going out onto the bowsprit to inspect the end of the spinnaker pole and get it ready for the resetting job.

SOMEBODY GOOFED. That is what usually happens when there's spinnaker trouble. A halyard is let go too soon, or is improperly cleated; someone allows a sheet to slip. Then panic, and/or an embarrassed flush around the ears that has nothing to do with sunburn.

EVERYTHING WENT AT ONCE on Sapphire—sheet, after guy and halyard —hardly the approved method of taking off a spinnaker. There'll be some laundry to dry after they get this one back on board.

WONDER WHAT WATERMELON'S SKIPPER is saying about this: spinnaker sheet flying off to leeward, pole standing nearly on end and fouling up the jib. Spectacular, but not seamanlike.

NEREUS *IS IN TROUBLE HERE.* Spinnaker halyard slipped several feet, dropping the kite onto the water where it is scooping up the 12-meter's bow wave. Working party clustered in bow had better get the spinnaker off the pole in a hurry before something goes "B-O-I-N-G!"

SPINNAKERS AT WORK. No trouble here; kites flying the way kites were meant to fly and doing the job they were built to do.

FASHION NOTE: The well-dressed International-6-Meter-Class yacht will wear square-shouldered, deep-chested spinnakers this season. Two modishly attired racers storm up to Seawanhaka Corinthian finish line with kites trimmed about as far forward as they can be carried.

GOOSE IN FULL FLIGHT. *Most famous of latter-day U. S. A. Sixes buzzes along in a fresh, quartering breeze, as very wet member of her crew, squatting on narrow, slippery foredeck, stops genoa jib to stay in preparation for next leg of the course.*

CRUISING CUTTER DEPARTURE II *plows a foaming furrow down Buzzards Bay under the pull of her perfectly set masthead spinnaker.*

J IBING A SPINNAKER, so that the yacht can carry the wind over the opposite quarter on the succeeding course, is a maneuver that requires nicely coordinated teamwork between the foredeck operator and those handling sheets and guys from the cockpit. Too much or too little strain on a line, any mistake in timing the swing, and presently a very unhappy and vocal skipper will be commenting on the lubberliness of his crew. Close quarters contribute to the tension—and confusion.

A SISTER SHIP, FINN MAC CUMHAILL, *does her plowing with the help of a plump red horse in the spinnaker traces.*

CRUISING YACHTS *(see page 110), broad-reaching down to the gas buoy, which they must round before sailing the next leg of the course, are getting ready to jibe. The leading boat is "free-wheeling" her spinnaker (swinging it around without the pole, which will be attached to the kite again after the mainsail has been jibed over), but somebody had better start taking in a little sheet.*

109

TCH, TCH, COMMODORE! How did Revonoc's spinnaker get itself all wrapped up in the balloon forestaysail? The skipper himself had to go forward to remedy this snafu, which isn't helping Revonoc's speed or the owner's blood pressure even a little bit.

THE INSIDE POSITION at the turn onto the next leg of the course can be
very important in situations like this. As these International One-Designs run
down to the mark on the port jibe, Number 10, clear astern of Numbers 11
and 18, swings over onto the new tack first, so as to drive into the weather
berth if the others turn too wide of the buoy and leave a hole for her.

ALAS FOR NUMBER 10'S PLANS, Number 11 doesn't leave any hole. She delays her jibe until her inside position is safe and then does it hurriedly—and raggedly—with plenty of room to spare inside the more smoothly operating Number 18. To keep from illegally running down the leaders, Number 10's skipper slows his boat by bringing his mainsail amidships. Meanwhile, his foredeck man can figure out what to do with that spinnaker pole, which appears to have lost contact with everything vital.

WHO SAYS *handling the spinnaker is a man's job? Pat Hinman, former national women's champion, eyes fixed aloft, alert and reacting to every flaw, keeps the kite full on an International. Concentration is essential to this task.*

ONCE IN A MILLION YACHT RACES something happens as spectacularly incredible as the spinnaker-lassoing of the yawl *Merry Maiden* by the pursuing sloop *Julie*. Once in a lifetime the event is properly recorded and documented. Because Rosy and his omnipresent camera were at the start of a New York Yacht Club race from Glen Cove to Port Jefferson, this singular example of unconventional yachting procedure was duly logged for posterity. The tragicomic story of one yacht towing another by the full length of an errant spinnaker and its halyard, stretched wire-taut between the mizzenmast truck of the tow*er* and the mainmast head of the towed, is told here.

"DOUBLE, DOUBLE TOIL AND TROUBLE." That's what Merry Maiden has here. Starting with her spinnaker set in an extraordinary, strangulated hourglass form, Merry Maiden, not moving too rapidly for that very reason, suddenly finds even this restrained progress slowed as though brakes had been applied. They had—in the form of Julie's spinnaker, which, loosed from all of its bonds save the bitter end of its halyard (someone had knotted that), soared out ahead of the sloop and entwined itself around a metal fitting atop Merry Maiden's mizzenmast. Meanwhile, the passing throng passes.

SINCE JULIE'S SPINNAKER refuses to unwrap itself and go elsewhere, one of Merry Maiden's crew goes aloft to end this impromptu demonstration of how strong a torn kite and a length of line can be. The passing continues.

MAN AT WORK—under difficulties. Standing on the jumper strut, knees pressed against the spar, he struggles with a bundle of billowing nylon, performing radical surgery with his seaman's knife. Note how the throng is thinning.

SUCCESS! Hacked and torn, slashed from its tenacious embrace on Merry Maiden's mizzen, away goes Julie's spinnaker, a problem now only to Julie's crew. Merry Maiden is free to do something about her own kite and the pursuit of opponents who passed her while she was in the towing business.

OUT OF STYLE NOW are the long bowsprits (or "nosepoles," as they are sometimes called), which were the lower terminals of the stays on which sailing yachts set their jibs and, not infrequently, dunking stools for hapless members of the crew at work on these exposed perches. When you see a bowsprit these days, it is a puny thing, indeed, compared to those which *Migrant, Hussar, Aloha* and the other departed big ones poked ahead of their bow waves. But long or short, round or flat, bowsprits are the working platforms for men who literally sail before the mast.

WALKING TIGHTROPES stretched between wind and water, Migrant's aerialist sailors furl her outer jib on the bowsprit's end.

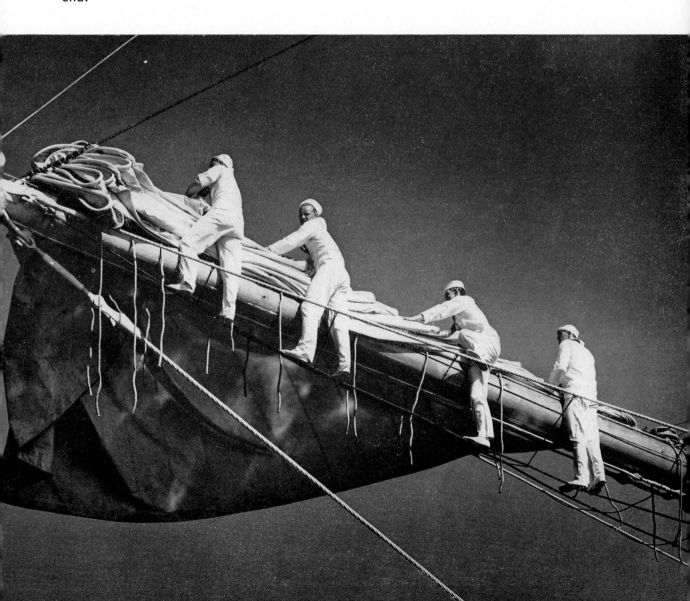

INFANTA'S BOWSPRIT *is the one-man-capacity type: one agile man. Here, wrapped around the jibstay so that he can devote two hands to his task, he unhanks the genoa jib and keeps it under control for the shipmate (hidden by the forestaysail) whose job it is to pull it aft.*

NINA'S BOWSPRIT *is very much shorter than* Migrant's *but no more comfortable for the men wrestling with the jib they doused before her reaching headsail was set. Now the problem is to get it back on deck without getting it wet. One deep curtsy by* Nina *will fix that—and them, too.*

JUST ONE MORE and the job is done. Like a monkey on a stick, Infanta's bowsprit lad stoops to free the snap shackle holding the jib tack in place. His mate, literally up to his neck in canvas, smothers the sail on the foredeck as Infanta slices her way to windward.

NO BOWSPRITS, no sails, but pictorially entrancing. This
quiet wharfside scene in Key West with the shrimping fleet at
rest is proof that beauty on the water is where the eye sees it.

TROUBLE IS WHAT YOU MAKE IT; and you can make plenty for yourself when you get careless with a spinnaker, as the crew of *Nisswa* learned the hard way one otherwise bright sailing day.

SOMEONE DID SOMETHING, or forgot to do something, with the spinnaker fore guy; so up the mast went the pole and into a state of collapse went the kite. All hands except the helmsman are forward to remedy the matter.

AH, THAT SITUATION is under control. Spinnaker pole is down where it belongs, fore guy cleated securely and the crew headed aft. But, Oops! Now what? More trouble. The spinnaker sheet's gone adrift. Wonder what the man at the helm is saying.

SO BACK TO THE FOREDECK goes the crew. The man in white lowers the pole's tip so that the others can grab the foot of the flopping spinnaker and fight it back into the boat, inch by inch, until the truant sheet is retrieved. Sailing is _such_ fun!

STIFF NECKS IN THE MAKING, as *Marilee's* crew assembles on fore-deck to try to clear jib halyard fouled aloft—and to watch. Meanwhile, the opposition goes past to windward.

YOU CAN JUST SEE overtaking yacht's spinnaker swelling past Marilee's mast, as her crew—all except man who apparently plans to do something about depressing inboard end of spinnaker pole—gazes aloft.

MORE SKY-GAZING, more bouncing on the pole, while smaller boat to windward makes hay— and distance.

THAT FASCINATING THING is still aloft, the heavyweight's down on deck again, without having budged the pole an inch, and the other boat is still gaining.

STATUS QUO. *Neck-craning convention still in progress on Marilee's fore-deck, burying her bow, hurting her speed. See how much NY 19 has gained since first picture?*

SOMETIMES IT JUST HAPPENS: a freak accident with no one at fault. The result, however, is the same: a disconcerting incident and no prize. Take the case of the yawl *Good News,* racing on Buzzards Bay one pleasant summer day.

IT WAS AN AFTERNOON such as this when Good News was slipping across the bay as pretty as you please with all of her light stuff set and drawing to a gentle northerly breeze when . . .

132

132

SUDDENLY THE WIND shifted ahead. It was "Up genoa jib, down spinnaker, and smartly, too!" The crew of Good News turned to with a will. The jib was run up the stay quickly and broken out; the spinnaker was cast off the pole preparatory to taking it down in the lee of the mainsail. But the spinnaker wouldn't come down; its halyard had jumped out of its sheave way up the tall mast and jammed there. So . . .

GOOD NEWS *sailed for miles with a man up her mast in a bos'n's chair work-ing to free the fouled halyard. Despite her troubles, Good News moved along, overtaking Circe and giving the latter's afterguard a box-seat view of the proceedings. Eventually the spinnaker was cleared; and, later in the day, when the sou'wester freshened to characteristic Buzzards Bay velocity . . .*

GOOD NEWS, *looking as she did on a luckier day when this photograph was made, went booming along to the finish line at an exhilarating pace with everything drumhead-taut and pulling like a twenty-mule team.*

EXTRANEOUS HAZARDS frequently are encountered in yacht racing on Long Island Sound, and not the least of them are the long tows of scows which ply between New York's concrete-mixing plants and the Island's seemingly inexhaustible sand pits. Tug skippers, by and large, cooperate with the racers as far as possible, within the limitations imposed by wind, tide, unwieldy barges and the fact that they're working, not playing, on the water. Occasionally, though, tows and racers arrive simultaneously at a channel buoy. When they do, a situation is likely to arise which, to state it conservatively, has a high confusion potential. For instance, the time that the 12-meter sloop *Gleam* and a long, double-width tow of deeply laden sand scows foregathered at Matinicock Point buoy. The tow was merely passing it en route to the East River; *Gleam* had to round the aid to navigation and change course to the northward. Too late, *Gleam* discovered that she just was not moving fast enough in the very light, following breeze to get around the bow of the tug, whose tow was being helped along by the flood tide. So, she jibed ship, trimmed in main and spinnaker and went for the stern of the tow, a few hundred yards to windward. This emergency attempt to carry a kite upwind precipitated the panic party pictured here.

THE TOW is just two barges too long (top, page 137). While Nina jibes her vast array of laundry and the yawl Sagola (right) just squeezes past the stern of the last scow in the string, Gleam sags down onto the third in line.

GLEAM bumps her topsides along the solid, rough planking of the scow (center, page 137), her crew dividing itself between the job of taking in the kite and fending off the sand-carrier.

ANOTHER MINUTE and she will be clear (bottom, page 137). One member of Gleam's crew moves onto the barge, the better to perform fending-off duties—which subsequently took him overboard. The tall cutter in the background is Nimrod V, which, with a little help from the harried tugboat captain, did get around the head of the tow. Leader of the fleet at the time, she was the only yacht that made it.

STUDIES IN CHARACTER CONTRASTS. You'd hardly know they were the same yachts; but different days, different weather impart entirely different personalities to sailing vessels.

STORMY WEATHER *is a name that ill-befits this limp, bedraggled object begging a capful of wind for its helpless sails.*

SAGOLA (*now Amigo and once Katuna*) *isn't much better off as she creeps along hoping that there's wind besides rain in those inky clouds.*

NOW LOOK AT STORMY, *slugging her way across the Gulf Stream in a two-reef breeze and a smother of white water—hard-bitten, tough.*

AND HERE'S SAGOLA *(Katuna then), lively and lovely as she can be; ra*
down, hard on the wind and going like Billy-O.

O N THE WIND, off the wind, across the wind: three different points of sailing are demonstrated by some of the ablest performers in the offshore fleet.

THE HEAVY-TONNAGE PART of the entry list, Class A, makes a windward start for Bermuda in 1952. Ketch Valkyrie has best position at the lee end of the line and leads fleet across. They pay off, though, on the finish. She wound up last in her class.

SQUARED OFF with the wind dead aft is this trio of campaigners. In the usual order: Argyll, Djinn and Burma.

WITH A CRACKING GOOD BREEZE *just abaft the beam, right where the yawls like it, Cotton Blossom IV, Djinn and Sea Lion gallop off on a broad reach.*

A JOB FOR THE SAILMAKER, *trouble for the crew. The 12-Meter Class had no sooner settled down after the start of a race on a sparkling, breezy day at Newport than Night Wind's spinnaker split right up the middle.*

AND SPEAKING OF FINISHES, how do you like this one between sloop
Gypsy and schooner Nina at Brenton Reef Lightvessel? Looks as though Nina
will win it by a nosepole; she has a bowsprit, Gypsy doesn't.

THE TWO BIG BLACK B'S, Baruna and Bolero (nearer camera) in one of the
many private duels they fought before Baruna made San Francisco her home
port and Bolero went under the Swedish flag. So closely matched were these
great ocean-going yawls that they once finished virtually lapped on each
other after racing 466 miles from Newport to Annapolis.

AIRY ARABELLA, *stepping along with head held high and flaunting a new striped parachute, was built as a family cruising ketch, but at the age of eighteen won a lockerful of prizes on the European circuit.*

HEY, SPINNAKER, *where are you going with that boat? Revonoc's huge kite, dwarfing hull and rest of rig, seems to be lifting her right out of the water.*

THE CREW'S WORK is never done, or so it seems to the weary bilgeboy. Here the race has started, spinnaker is set and drawing nicely and the "cheater" (impolite nickname for the little triangular sail rigged to fill in the gap under the parachute) is doing its job. Instead of sitting down and contemplating the beauties of this scene, Djinn's forward deck personnel is hoisting and stopping the genoa in preparation for the next leg, and those neck-craners at the mast are sighting along it to see whether it contains any wobbles or hooks.

FIRST LIGHT in the forest—the bare forest made by the masts of the Off Soundings Club fleet snugged down in New London. All's quiet below and not a soul is stirring on the piers; but, when the sun is a little higher, everything will come alive for the first run of the cruise.

DAWN IN MAINE (see page 154). You can almost scent the heady Down East blend of balsam and rockweed in this daybreak picture of Salisbury Cove.

WHETHER THEY ARE IN QUEST OF THRILLS that only a tussle with Nature in her own arena can provide, seeking escape from the frets and frustrations of shorebound existence, or unashamedly succumbing to the lure of what Longfellow called the "beauty and mystery of the ships and the magic of the sea," none can deny that increasing thousands of bankers and bakers and candlestick-makers—and oft-times their ladies—are adopting sailing as their sport.

Whatever the motivation, they find it a fascinating, compelling avocation, one whose grip becomes unyielding, almost impossible to break. Once caught in the toils of sea and sail, only a few return to what the land offers.

For sailing sings a siren song, a ballad of ever-changing tempo, of mood and emphasis as varied as the winds themselves. The thunder of an ugly black squall one minute, the majestic tones of a rainbow-streaked sky the next. The pure, joyous melody of a lovely little ship flitting through sun-flecked seas; the somber dissonance of one slatting in a greasy calm. The racy, spine-tingling allegro of a split-second start in a lively breeze; and the groaning, Wagnerian rumbling of lubberly execution.

There are fast passages and slow; keen races and dull drifting matches; fair weather and foul; lucky puffs and unlucky shifts; happy incidents and others which the principals are not eager to repeat. This is sailing: gaiety and laughter, disappointment and despair, drama and minor tragedy, good fellowship and a tot of grog when the hook's down—excitement and beauty which the landsman cannot know.

These are the diverse elements that Rosy sought to capture on film when he and his boys put to sea in *Foto*, sighting his lens on the familiar, the strange; snapping something of passing importance, something of lasting; for that was his job, his daily bread. It was his hobby, his art, too. So he never missed an opportunity for creative and interpretive camera work.

He derived professional satisfaction from photographing a spectacular start. He glowed inside when he caught something which he felt was a breath of the true spirit of sailing, something as elusive, as quickly fleeting as the change of sun and shadow on the noiseless, curving wings of wind-driven ships.

In these remaining pages we shall see more of Rosy the reportorial photographer, more of Rosy the marine artist and more of his masterworks.

W HO DURST BE SO BOLD with a few crooked boards nailed together, a stick standing upright and a rag tied to it, to adventure into the ocean?" So asked one Thomas Fuller early in the seventeenth century. He has his answer generally in the thousands of men who go down to the sea in cruising yachts, and specifically in the crews of the little ships that made these subjects for Rosy's camera.

A ROSENFELD CLASSIC: Big Sea, Little Boat. Sloop Larry, reefed down in a strong breeze, jumps her forefoot clear out of water, as the Atlantic gives her the roller coaster treatment.

VIVA LOS HABANEROS! Cuba's pride, and most successful of its ocean racers, the yawl Criollo, engaged in her favorite occupation—galloping to windward in a fresh breeze. She's driving out from under the fleet shortly after the start of the 1957 Miami-to-Nassau race, in which she was first to finish and tops in her class.

UNDINA, Bermuda's contribution to the ocean racing fleet, lifts out of a Gulf Stream sea and cascades it down her decks as she drives toward another.

SIZE IS NOT ESSENTIAL to success in ocean racing. Finisterre, four inches less than 39 feet in overall length, won, among numerous other honors, the Southern circuit championship and the 50th Anniversary Bermuda fixture in 1956 . . .

ANOTHER OCEAN CHAMPION is the yawl Mare Nostrum. Then under the Spanish flag, but now once more under the American, she won the trans-Atlantic race to San Sebastian and was first around the Fastnet course in 1955. Husky, handsome and powerful is this big 'un of the blue-water flotilla.

AND MALAY, named for the 45-foot schooner that prevailed in 1930, took
the Bermuda Trophy in 1954 and the Halifax prize the following year.
Malay, yawl-rigged like Finisterre, is a foot longer. No smaller yacht than
these ever won the race from the U. S. A. to the Onion Patch.

AND SO IS THE LARGER YAWL WINDIGO on the other tack.
Wet going but fast, and the sort of sailing that makes the
heart beat a little quicker, the spine tingle with the thrill of it.

BOW WAVE SHATTERING ITSELF into foam on the lee rail, Caribbee, queen of the Southern Seas before the advent of Hoot Mon and Finisterre, is the picture of power as she drives to windward . . .

ALL OF THE SAILING isn't done in the summertime, under warm southern skies or in big boats. Hundreds of little dinghies, manned by sailing folk who revel in their classification as "Frostbiters," race throughout the winter in frigid Long Island Sound, Narragansett Bay and Massachusetts ports. Theirs is a happy breed: immune to pneumonia, scornful of plunging thermometers and unmindful of the icy baths that await capsizers.

SNOW PUT AN AUTHENTIC BITE in the frost for these Frostbiters, so intent on wondering who is going to have an overlap on whom when they get to the turning flag that they ignore the falling flakes.

ACTION IS AS BRISK as is the weather. Responsive, lively Class B and Interclub dinks turn the windward mark (hidden somewhere under the sails of 55 or 25) and ease sheets for the run inshore.

SOMETHING IS ALWAYS HAPPENING to *Gleam*. If the facts were not well known to be otherwise, she might be suspected of being a vessel that had been launched on a Friday, changed her name and sailed on her maiden voyage on a Sunday. When she isn't sticking herself on Hedge Fence shoal, having her troubles with the turbulent tides and with wandering anchor-draggers in Edgartown Harbor or bouncing off barges in Long Island Sound, she spills members of her crew overboard. But she gets them back. Here's the sad story in pictures of how impromptu aquatics by a crew member cost *Gleam* a possible victory over her 12-Meter rival, *Vim*.

JUST BEFORE THE CRY of "Man over-board!" went up from Gleam's deck, she was slipping along under spin-naker and pulling slowly but steadily away from Vim. Vim had jibed over to bring the wind on her starboard quarter, so Gleam mustered her fore-deck hands to do likewise.

"SO QUICK bright things come to confusion." A lad who had been helping to move the spinnaker pole across the deck was kicked overboard by it. Here he snuggles up to the life ring that had been tossed to him; while, in the distance, his shipmates struggle to get the errant spinnaker under control, trim in the mainsail and begin rescue operations.

THE SITUATION is now under control. Gleam luffs up alongside her involuntary deserter and a line is heaved to him.

STRONG AND WILLING HANDS haul him aboard, life ring and all.

WHEW! That's over. While the erstwhile swimmer sits on the deck for a moment to get his breath, the rest of the crew turns to on the job of setting off in pursuit of the now long-since-departed Vim.

SOMETIMES THIS "MAN OVERBOARD!" BUSINESS is done in whole-sale lots, as in the case of mass immersion superinduced by the capsize of a stricken Raven Class sloop. Then three lads and a gal experience shipwreck and rescue.

THIS IS HOW IT BEGAN. Vinky was speeding along on the downwind leg of a race with everything as pretty as you please when . . .

A HEAVY PUFF gave her just the added impetus to get her onto a plane.
Raven Vinky flew for several lengths like this, until . . .

BANG! The spinnaker sheet snapped and the kite took charge. The main was quickly eased and . . .

ALL HANDS—except the helmsman, who has shifted to the weather side and is fighting to keep the boat off the wind—move forward to take in the spinnaker. But another heavy puff hits and . . .

173

OVER SHE GOES! That's all for Vinky.

RESCUE is quickly at hand. While Vinky's crew stands, kneels or reclines on her overturned hull (wooden centerboard boats float when they capsize and make convenient life rafts), a cabin cruiser steams up to salvage racer and crew.

THE TRUE ARTIST IN ROSY emerges in those moments when sun, clouds, water and sails join forces for the blink of an eyelid to form a perfect picture.

Here are a few examples. The moods are different; so are the yachts and backgrounds involved; but the end results are the same— marine portraiture at its superlative best.

THE WESTERING SUN, glowing through a heavy cloudbank over the Connecticut shore, silhouettes sloop, yawl and ketch in almost a moonlight effect as they sail eastward in a soft evening breeze.

THE GLOOM of a drenching rain squall envelops these little sloops, groping for the finish line of a Larchmont Yacht Club race over waves flattened by the downpour.

A CHRISTMAS CARD for Rosy. Every year Mr. Rosenfeld selects one of his better studies for his personal greeting card. In 1956 it was the sloop Hustler, flying down a boisterous northwest breeze to victory in a Manhasset Bay race.

GOLDEN SUNLIGHT, *fluffy cumulus clouds and shimmering, dancing water frame Ticonderoga, all alone in this bejeweled setting. Days like these at sea more than compensate the sailor for the woes and worries of his game and make windjamming converts of plow jockeys.*

SUNSET ON THE SOUND—*Long Island Sound—finds Gesture (left) and* Nereus *nursing the last of a dying breeze, barely making steerage way toward the home port to windward, and probably quite unaware—and unappreciative—of what a lovely picture they make.*

THREE OF A KIND with the same goal: get to the finish line before the other. Forty-foot Concordia yawls, Niam, Crisette and Rusta IV, as alike in hull and sail as sparrows on a wire, racing in New York Yacht Club port-to-port run on Buzzards Bay.

GEORGE ADE once advised those who would insure their peace of mind to ignore the rules and regulations. He could not have had yacht racers in mind; for when they pay no heed to the code they get protests, not peace. And protests are usually followed by hearings and hearings by punishment—that is, if the protestor can present the necessary convincing evidence. In this case, the evidence was the pictures you are going to see, and their story was so eloquently convincing that the guilty party was disqualified.

It happened in a Two-Ten Class start off Larchmont and involved what is termed barging, that is, a windward boat's bearing off on one to leeward in order to squeeze into a nonexistent aperture on the proper side of the starting flag, or failing to sail higher when required to do so by a leeward yacht.

OPUS I (85), sheets eased and barging most egregiously at the weather end of the starting line, suddenly discovers that the black boat coming across her bows close hauled isn't going to let her in.

MEANWHILE the white boat next to leeward of Opus (it is Harpoon, Number 2) is going to have a spot of trouble responding to the higher course of Allegra (Number 138), which is well overlapped on her lee quarter.

OPUS is forced to the wrong side of the starting flag; and there's Harpoon, sheets slacked off and sails luffing, on the line but paying no mind to Allegra, which has right to sail higher but cannot because Harpoon is in the way.

WHILE OPUS JIBES around to make a new start, Harpoon bumps Allegra's weather side. You can see gal in Harpoon's cockpit pushing off Allegra's bow and the only man in Allegra's crew holding off Harpoon's backstay, and imagine what Allegra's skipper is saying.

FOUL! Girl in plaid shorts prepares to break out red code flag B in Allegra's shrouds, to indicate that Allegra will protest Harpoon's action. Harpoon went on with the race only to get the heave-ho from the protest committee after judicial proceedings.

HANDLING SMALL BOATS under spinnakers in a hard, knockdown-laden breeze, such as a typical cool northwester on Long Island Sound, is anything but a pastime for the timid soul or faint heart.

Rosy was on hand to record this exciting duel between *Spellbound* (Number 13, dark hull) and *Dodger* (Number 15, light hull) on a day when the International One-Designs were traveling at or near hull speed all the way down a leeward leg that was sailed almost in less time than it takes to tell the story. Mast, rigging and crew are under heavy strain in such going.

Spellbound emerged from the scuffle in first place, but subsequent gear failures dropped her to third at the finish. When she arrived there she was informed that she wasn't in the race after all: She had crossed the starting line before the gun, failed to heed the recall and so was disqualified. There is nothing in yacht racing that quite matches the sense of utter frustration that engulfs skippers to whom race committees break this sad news.

HERE THEY ARE storming down to the turning mark. Spellbound, *dragging her quarter wave almost on board, has set jib preparatory to dousing spinnaker.*

DODGER *has her jib set inside spinnaker now, too; and third*
boat has gained on two leaders.

A MOMENT LATER Dodger *squares away and* Spellbound *pulls ahead.*

A CLOSE CALL. Dodger, *hit with a savage puff, comes up*
harply, just missing Spellbound's *stern.*

SPELLBOUND *has the inside track as the boats reach the turning mark; and white boat is just outside of Dodger as they trim sheets for beat to finish.*

THEIR NAMES meant something—and still do—to those who regard our ocean racing fleet as the keeper of the keys of America's great sailing tradition. Whether they were winners or those that never quite made the bolder headlines, they were great ships, well and truly sailed, making their contributions in their own special ways to the sport of men unashamed to reveal themselves as idealists.

AVANTI IS GONE NOW—mangled, tortured, then torn apart in Hurricane Carol. Rosy caught her here as the sprightly, pulsating, living thing she was when this lovely yawl settled down to a thrash to windward in a whole sail breeze.

SHE'S BEEN AROUND, has Doris—around the Southern circuit, around the English coast for the Fastnet and such, and around Bermuda and New England waters—first as Elizabeth McCaw, affectionately dubbed "Lizzie Mac" by those who sailed in her, and then as Doris. Built as a cruiser, she responded like a thoroughbred when they took her to the races.

MISTRESS IS A LADY (see page 194), a very well-traveled lady of the sea, under whose leaden keel many thousands of miles of salt water have flowed. Nine Bermuda races; one to Plymouth, England; and one to Bergen, Norway, are among the passages logged under racing conditions by the first schooner built to the Cruising Club of America rule of measurement.

CIRCE IS ANOTHER YAWL who'd rather have it piping up than otherwise (see page 195). Here the long-legged, slim-waisted beauty is getting just the opposite. So she's just slithering along, following her high-flown kite across this pictorially beautiful but lifeless sea.

193

VALKYRIE, *shown here with the now infrequently used jib topsail, was one of the sturdy, wind-eating big ketches that could make the water fly when she set out to chew her way up a good breeze and a lump of sea.*

FOR SHEER LOVELINESS *it would be difficult, if not impossible, to match this portrait of Marie Amelie, ex-Onkahya, a lady of the Lakes who used to winter in Florida before a new admirer took her to Southern California and then on a long sail to Honolulu.*

NO HEAVY HAND needed here; just a gentle, sensitive finger or two on the wheelspokes to keep Djinn gliding daintily down the path of wind and sun.

BELLE OF THE WEST, lifted by a heaving sea, is all for taking the bit in her teeth and shying up to windward of her course. But her helmsman, feet braced against the lee cockpit seat, both hands horsing the tiller up into his lap, has a tight rein on her.

ALWAYS ONE OF THOSE you have to beat if you aspire to cups and bowls and plates of silver is Argyll, as tough as the clansmen from the Scottish shire for which she was named, as lovely as the lochs and glens from whence came her inspiration.

FROM THE SHOALS of old Nantucket, her island hailing port, to the coral islets of the Bahamas, Sea Lion has campaigned, liking it best when the going was hardest. A fresh breeze was wine in her cup.

VOYAGE'S END for Bermuda races—entrance to St. George's Harbor and, in the distance to seaward, the committee boat standing its lonely finish-line vigil.

VOYAGE'S END for the cruiser (see page 204)—sails furled, hook down in a quiet anchorage at sundown.

I T DOESN'T TAKE A BIG BOAT to make a big picture. A fairly small
one will be more than adequate in the right circumstances.

FOR INSTANCE, this Atlantic Class sloop driving hard in an
effort to beat an onrushing squall in a race to the finish line.

COMMERCE AND PLEASURE use the same water highways, sometimes with the results shown here: the big and little of it. You couldn't pose a picture such as this made by a freighter, inbound to New York for cargo, thrusting her bulk between the leaders in a tight International Class race.

IN THEIR DAY, now two decades past, the Sound Interclubs made many a stirring picture thumping across blustery nor'westers, with Aileen (Number 25) leading the embattled pack.

AS OCEAN RACERS GO, Starlight (Number 46) is on the small side; but neither big wind nor big sea nor big opponents could daunt her when racing bent.

AILING ISN'T ALL frenzied action and suspense in close quarters racing. It isn't all long, wearying wheel watches on a hard passage. It isn't all fun and frolic, all work and wet clothes.

SOMETIMES it is the pleasant pre-regatta chores and chit-chat of race day on the yacht club lawn.

AND SOMETIMES *it is slipping
into a lovely, peaceful haven
like New London Harbor.*

SOMETIMES IT IS MERELY APPRECIATING the throat-catching beauty of the sea around us: its ships, its shores, its inspirations to poet and artist alike.

"AND SOME DAY, when skies are fair,
Up the bay my ship will sail."

"*SO DIES a wave along the shore,*
Its last caress from the eternal sun."